Brian Robinson

Be Hopeful
Brian Robins

The **MI OWN** *Collection*

Volume I: Therapeutically Traveling Through Time,
FOR HIM

D1279705

The MI OWN Collection
Volume I: Therapeutically Traveling Through Time, For Him

Published by Literacy in Motion Phoenix, Arizona
www.AnthonyThigpen.com
www.PaideiaTribune.com

Anthony KaDarrell Thigpen Editor-in-Chief

Library of Congress Cataloging-in-Publication Data Publisher and Printing by Literacy in Motion
Cover Design by Netsys Interactive, Inc., James Day, *Creative Director*

The MI OWN Collection
Volume I: Therapeutically Traveling Through Time, For Him
ISBN: 978-1-7336583-2-4

Self-Help/Sci-fi
Printed in the United States of America

Acknowledgements & Dedication

Latin philosopher René Descartes said, "**I think, therefore I am**". I know who I am: I am a collection of *Mi Own* thoughts. Who are you? I dedicate this book to every person on the journey of discovering a greater sense of self-awareness and self-worth - you are important.

The following individuals worked together as a unit to help me therapeutically travel through time during my process of publishing this book: My dad, mom and brother, Brian, Tammy and Myles Robinson; my grandparents, Clary and Patsy Butler, my aunt Cora Butler and my avuncular, of Literacy in Motion publishing, Anthony KaDarrell Thigpen.

Thank you God
Sent from **Mi**-Phone

TABLE OF *CONCEPTS*

Section 1

THE MI OWN COLLECTION

Volume 1: Therapeutically Traveling Through Time, For Him

Section 1
MI OWN THOUGHTS

Thought 1
THE SEARCH FOR MEANING
The Genius in Me

T his man was a genius. He was a genius intellectually. He was a genius creatively. He was a genius by nature. According to his peers, he was a highly favored intellectual with a fantastic brain, yet seemingly unusual. He was personable and social, ate healthy and drank only what was good for his body. He exceled and experienced success in whatever fields of work he chose. However, even with all his charisma and gifts, he was never truly happy. He worked tirelessly; living with absolute purpose while putting forward his best effort. Nonetheless, he never found meaning in his work. In effort to understand himself better and find meaning in his own life, he set out on a mission. His goal was to explore every known dimension of life – specifically his own. Ultimately, he aimed to discover the perfect balance between purpose and meaning – he wanted to discover happiness.

The man started his journey by attempting to understand the people around him. He tried to take the best pieces from the fragmented lives of others in order to improve upon his own life – only to quickly discover that he was traveling on broken pieces. He rapidly discovered the difference between reality verses perception. Yet, this journey remained his new drive – his new mission. A mission that sparked a sense of excitement everyday! He woke up and searched adamantly for new people, studying their behaviors in order to understand his own life. Unfortunately, as his understanding became greater, he wanted to know people less. He became more depressed and anxious than when he first set out on his journey. So, he decided to make a change. He was no longer interested in how people found happiness, but he became infatuated with trying to understand why people were so happy in the first place. He set out to discover the meaning of life by writing – jotting down incomplete thoughts daily until each piece completed a different section of life's puzzle. From his own outside perspective, he wrote the meaning of life. Each thought was based on his own understanding of the individuals he encountered. Admittedly, he wasn't a good writer, but he tried. His thoughts were far too jumbled and extreme for others to understand. In effort to script his scattered thoughts on paper he named his first unpublished collection of concepts, *Homeless*. The initial journey made him feel more vulnerable than anticipated, but it also created a sense of mental clarity.

Homeless had no place in this world. How could he expect anyone to understand his own fragmented thoughts, if he could make no sense them himself? He was frustrated by his lack of self-awareness and understanding. However, writing about his passions made him more passionate. As a result, he continued his search for knowledge, despite being misunderstood. The journey started in his mind. It seemed the more he asked, "Why," the less he understood. He learned that every person in life had a different reason for being happy. As a result, understanding others wasn't the fuel he needed to launch him to the next dimension of life. He desperately wanted to get to a place of happiness. This destination required him to deal with his own cluttered dimension, as jumbled and confused as his own thoughts within this space might be. In order to get to the better place, he had to sort through his homeless thoughts. He called these thoughts homeless because they were too difficult to comprehend. This extreme mental, emotional and social confusion made him feel anxious, stressed and vulnerable.

Therefore, young genius decided to disconnect from reality – only for a short time. He felt suspended in space, but it seemed necessary in order to to reach his own happiness. So, to get to the dimension called *Happy*, he changed his focus. He understood with clarity that people were capable of great things. Yet, he was confident that people have so much more potential than they perceived. Individuals need only believe in themselves – believe in past human achievements – believe in the better future.

Now, he wanted to know if humanity would ever reach its

endless potential. He figured that if the people of this present day were always improving themselves, then maybe his life would be better in a future world. So, the man, being one of the most creative minds, decided to build a time machine. Much like all other fields of work he explored, he was successful. It took away some of his youthful glow to do something so extreme; but for the first time in a while, he was filled with purpose again. Still, he continued searching for meaning. So, building the time machine wasn't enough. He had to use it in order to find the truth he was looking for. He desired to see what life would be like hundreds of years into the future. So, he set the machine to 200 years and vanished from the only world he once knew.

The Mi Own Collection is the treasure chest of collaborative thoughts, which are pieced together by each reader in their individual journals. Individuals are able to therapeutically travel through time to understand their own reality as it relates to the world around them.

MI OWN JOURNAL

Use this MI OWN journal section to write your own thoughts concerning **YOUR SEARCH FOR MEANING**, *there is a genius inside of you waiting to be discovered.*

Thought 2
LOOK INTO THE FUTURE
Stay Woke

When the man awoke, he was in a heap of trash. Somehow, he instantly knew that his time travels had been successful. The trash was more advanced than anything he had ever imagined. He looked around and found wonderful things: He saw trash that defied gravity, trash that regenerated on its own, even trash that was transparent – and nearly invisible. He would've stayed in the trash heap forever, trying to only find the meaning behind what other people had already used. Instead, he ventured onward to complete his quest. All he brought to this amazing future world was an empty notebook and a pencil. He had no tools to understand the amazing trash he was surrounded by. In order to understand the mysteries of the future that he had landed in, he left the trash behind and continued his journey.

MI OWN JOURNAL

Use this MI OWN journal section to write your own thoughts concerning **LOOKING INTO THE FUTURE,** *how do you envision and feel about your future?*

_____

_____

_____

_____

_____

Thought 3
CLIMBING THE MOUNTAIN
The Heap of Trash

Once the man was out of the heap of trash, he realized that he was at the bottom of a large hill. Luckily, he saw a sign. The sign was able to telepathically communicate to the man just from him visually recognizing the symbols that the sign displayed. Instantly, the sign transported a message whereas he knew that everything he was looking for was at the top of the hill. It simply said, Dr. Hope – Historian. The man needed strength to climb from the bottom to the top – from the heap of trash to the mountain of hope. It was a perfect inspirational sign. It served as motivation for the man to start his uphill journey. It's important to note that the sign was so futuristic that the genius could've stayed stuck forever trying to decode the intricate mechanisms of the sign. Instead, focused on finding what he was looking for, he followed the road up the hill.

MI OWN JOURNAL

Use this MI OWN journal section to write your own thoughts concerning **CLIMBING THE MOUNTAIN,** *by identifying your own mountain of hope.*

_____

_____

_____

_____

_____

_____

Thought 4

THE SCARY DOOR

Futuristic, Functional and Familiar

Once the man made it to the top of the hill he saw a house. At first, he thought that the house was far too futuristic to be functional. As he got closer, the house became explicitly detailed and clear – it was as if the house came alive. It was frightening. The house seemed so big, so complex, and so confusing; it had awkward entrances, one-sided windows, and rooms with inconsistent changing shapes. He saw colossal columns, awkward sculptures, statues, and blinding bright lights that caused his heart to race. He had no clue what would happen once he walked inside. Suddenly, as he approached, the front door appeared to be the same as the door of his own home – suddenly calming and inviting. In that moment, he felt comfortable enough to enter. Initially, he had to figure out how to get inside. Suddenly, he sensed it – it was simple! Just like guests entered his own house is how he would enter this place of shelter. He simple needed to knock.

MI OWN JOURNAL

Use this MI OWN journal section to write your own thoughts concerning **THE SCARY DOOR,** *whether futuristic, functional or familiar. What does the door mean to you?*

_____

_____

Thought 5

MEETING HOPE

Finding Answers

U pon knocking on the scary door, he found what he was looking for – he discovered what he needed. He encountered a person who could answer all of his questions. This person had the answers to every question concerning the man's past. He also possessed a picture perfect understanding about the futuristic world. He found Dr. Hope, the historian. The historian, ironically looked just like the man himself, yet an older version, who possessed far more wisdom. It was as if he was looking through a futuristic reflection. Of course, the man didn't see it that way through his own vantage point. He immediately started explaining his own perspective. After ranting on-and-on, his repetitive speech slowed to a screeching halt. "Will you answer some questions for me," the man asked Dr. Hope? "Of course," replied the historian. The doctor was more than happy to answer all the questions the man had. So, Dr. Hope let the man inside his futuristic home.

MI OWN JOURNAL

Use this MI OWN journal section to write your own thoughts concerning **MEETING HOPE,** *this dimension is about finding answers. What unanswered questions do you have about life?*

_____

_____

_____

Thought 6
ASK QUESTIONS, ANSWER QUESTIONS
Understanding Self

The first question the man asked the doctor was simple. "Why is your name Hope," he asked with curiosity? The man wanted to know if Dr. Hope was human, an inspirational manifestation or the creator of hope himself.

The doctor responded.

"My name is very common in this time," he said. "In the time before mine, my name was made to have a lot of meaning, but here it is just a name."

He explained that people of the future only care about the character of the person, not names or titles. In the future, your name only carries as much weight as your actions.

As the man felt more comfortable, he asked every question he could about the heap of trash where he first found himself. He wanted to understand all the fascinating wonders that the future world had to offer. Yet, every question led to another question. Dr. Hope was able to effectively answer every question the man could think to ask. The historian explained the answers with better clarity than the genius could ever hope to re-explain in his own words. However, eventually, the genius grew weary of the endless cycle of questions and answers. The hopeful historian remained patient, prepared and passionate about answering more questions. So the man, annoyed with the circle of relentless questions and answers, asked, "How are you so smart?" He stated that Dr. Hope must be the smartest man in the entire universe. On the other hand, Dr. Hope, the historian, responded with humility and patience. Dr. Hope's response was simple, "I am not nearly the smartest person in the universe, nor am I nearly the least smart. I am merely good at answering your questions." The man remained flustered by the endless stream of knowledge that Dr. Hope had as a historian. The man remained convinced that there could be none smarter than he. The man said, "No one individual could have so many answers without already knowing everything in the world." Dr. Hope kindly responded with indescribable humility. He stated, "Just like the knowledge you gained in your time, my knowledge came from my teachers. However, all the people of my time, and yours, are filled with great knowledge and a unique perspective of the world that they live in. I have chosen to learn from every person I encounter. The people of this world have chosen to learn from me. That is the only reason I am able to understand so much."

MI OWN JOURNAL

Use this MI OWN journal section to write your own thoughts concerning **ASK QUESTIONS, ANSWER QUESTIONS,** *this will help you to understand self. Despite your uncertainties, what are you certain about concerning your life?*

Thought 7

GOOD, BETTER, BEST
A New Way of Thinking

The man started to understand secrets things. He grasped hold of the source fueling the wisdom of Dr. Hope. Although the man still had many questions, his next question led to more clarity than any previous answer had given. Instead of asking how the things of the future worked, he asked, "Why are the people of *Mi Own* time not close to discovering such amazing things."

The historian applauded him for asking such an important question. Afterward, he proceeded to answer, His answer was clear and informative enough for the man to write down his own thoughts, in his own words. He said, "The reason why your time is so far from this better world is simple. Here in the future, we have changed our way of thinking. In your time, people fall into three categories, although they all live within each category at some point in their lives. They are either a student, a teacher, or a critic. The critic compares his or her life to that of another, whereas the student and the teacher both help each other improve. In this world we don't believe in critics. As a result, we can all believe that we are good at everything, without having any bad to compare good too. This new way of thinking has allowed all people to pursue their passion, without fear of judgment. We believe that the possibilities for mankind are truly endless and exciting."

MI OWN JOURNAL

Use this MI OWN journal section to write your own thoughts concerning **GOOD, BETTER, BEST,** *explore a new way of thinking.*

_____

_____

_____

_____

_____

_____

_____

_____

_____

_____

_____

_____

_____

_____

_____

_____

_____

_____

_____

_____

_____

_____

_____

_____

_____

_____

_____

Thought 8
TREE CLIMBING FOR FISH
Good Without Bad

T o the man, the *"Good, Better, Best"* way of thinking seemed easier said than done. So, he asked, "How could people truly be good without bad?" The historian, once again, responded with wisdom and clarity. "In this future, we don't believe in bad, we have instead replaced the word bad with the theory of better. The reason you believe in bad, and I do not embrace the very concept, has everything to do with your upbringing. The word goes back to our earliest teachers in life. In your time, the school systems taught you the concept of bad as early as you could understand it. For your generation, teaching people the concept of bad as a comparison to good created the idea of normal. The people of your time believe that normal people are not bad, but truthfully, normality stops people from being purely good. Our teachers believe in good and better. Comparing good and better creates no standard; it allows people to be creative. Unfortunately, in your time, creativity was rare. As a historian, I became aware that creativity was lacking in your time, due to your early education. An example that we understand from your school systems is based on essay writing.

When young children are instructed to write 80-100 words, most of them will write "80-100 words". In your time, that is considered wrong. The teachers are looking for expected results and will not compromise from the normal or traditional standard. Here in my time, we encourage students to liberate their minds. Students in your time are often told that their way of thinking is wrong. Your teachers say there is a wrong way and correct way of doing things. However, that isn't the case here. Their way wasn't wrong, it was just a different way. The teachers of our time don't criticize the different way, we just decide if it was a better way or not. Through that search for better, creativity is born, we escape from the idea of bad.

Unfortunately, your generation gave birth to the concept of bad. You teach right and wrong to children, not *Good, Better, Best*. The child that goes a different way is forced back on a path of normality and scolded for being different. So, the next time he sees a question like that on a paper he doesn't think of a new way to answer the problem, he just answers the question in the same fashion as everyone else. He's been taught to believe that's how it should be done. His creativity is reduced to nearly nothing – normality. He will go through life the same way as everyone else in order to squeeze his existence into the shoebox-sized standard of society. For us, there is no standard. We have no critics, and we believe in *Good, Better, Best*; which changes everything in this dimension.

MI OWN JOURNAL

Use this MI OWN journal section to write your own thoughts concerning **TREE CLIMBING FOR FISH,** *experiencing good without bad.*

Thought 9
ALL GOOD NO EVIL
A Picture of Reality

The man was puzzled and perplexed by the picture of this futuristic reality that Dr. Hope presented. He pondered how an entire society could have learned to be purely good. So he asked next, "How does this future world teach perfect goodness?" Dr. Hope responded with a profound truth.

"We believe that the idea of good is unique to each individual. The greatest minds of my time, from religious upbringings to scientific success, assembled to examine the bare basics behind the validity of perfect good. After weeks of discussion, they came to a consensus and divided good into three main parts. These three parts became the baseline for what we teach in our schools. It also added clarity for our teachers; enriching their understanding and empowering their profession. The three main parts of good are as follows; *Mi own, Yougwhay,* and *Endamily.* Each one of these parts are not purely good, but they help to understand the most relevant aspects about what is good itself."

MI OWN JOURNAL

Use this MI OWN journal section to write your own thoughts concerning **Good, Better, Best,** *explore a new way of thinking.*

_____

_____

_____

Thought 10
WHAT IS MI OWN?
Personalized Learning Experience

Mi own starts at the beginning of every lesson. Understanding *Mi Own* has everything to do with the ability to process your own individual thoughts. It is a culmination of processing information for *Me, Myself,* and *I* without the crutches, dependency and reliance of others. It is a futuristic and independent concept of understanding life on your own. Hence, *Mi Own* is an elevated perspective of thinking. *Mi Own* is the first phase of approaching all things that are good. For example, every new perspective starts with my own understanding, and each individual has *Mi Own* way of thinking – *Mi Own* is personal.

What needs to be improved? What are the goals? Who needs to be heard? These types of questions must be answered by keeping *Mi Own* at the forefront of the dialog. This is the first level of understanding – *Mi Own* understanding. Dr. Hope said, "In your time, most people memorize prior to learning. They don't know the basics of their own perspectives. Memorization is your first phase of learning. As a result, the people of your time are confused and become unhappy with their teaching." This is why *Mi Own* is crucial and the first main part of good.

MI OWN JOURNAL

Use this MI OWN journal section to write your own thoughts concerning **WHAT IS MI OWN,** *your personalized learning experience.*

Thought 11

Who is Yougwhay?

Yougwhay represents the time between the beginning and the end of anything in existence. Every lesson learned lies between the beginning and the end of class. Just like the important pages lie between the beginning and the end of a book – never judge a book by its cover. Every book, just like every lesson, leads us to a better understanding of various topics. However, the journey we take to arrive at the same finish line may be completely different – Yougwhay is about individual choices. The reason we have chosen to call the middle Yougwhay is because it is comprised of *you* and the *way* or *why* you intend to go to your destination. The letter "G" in the middle of the word Yougwhay is what makes the word unique. Life is not merely about doing things *your way* or influencing everyone to embrace *your why*. The letter "G" changes everything. Many people pronounced the "G" differently. For others the enunciation of the letter is completely silent. The letter "G" represents your *great* mind that defines individual perspectives. Yougwhay is the second or middle part of all things that are good.

MI OWN JOURNAL

Use this MI OWN journal section to write your own thoughts concerning **WHO IS YOUGWHAY?** *Embrace every aspect of your life's journey.*

Thought 12
WHERE IS ENDAMILY?

Endamily comes at the end. In fact, it is a combination of two major words; endless and family. It is our motivation for doing the things we do. However, it is also the reason why living things must come to an end. Dr. Hope said, "The people of my world don't fear Endamily, because it allows for Mi Own and Yougwhay to exist. We know, ideally, that all three of them are just parts of the greater good. If we chose to hate the end, then we are choosing to hate the beginning and the middle. So, in this world, we chose not to hate. For this reason, we are able too fully enjoy life; loving everything within it. Endamily is the third main part of good.

MI OWN JOURNAL

Use this MI OWN journal section to write your own thoughts concerning **WHERE IS ENDAMILY –** *the endless family.*

Thought 13
1,2,3

In more recent years, the three parts of good, *Mi Own*, Yougwhay and Endamily have just been numbered as the 1, the 2, and the 3. This makes it more relatable in the classroom settings. Everything you did before you take a class is considered the 1; everything you do in class is considered the 2; and what you gain after taking the class is considered the 3. Breaking down the learning experience into three basic components allows each individual to embrace a more enriching perspective. In addition, it also allows teachers to understand the student more holistically.

MI OWN JOURNAL

Use this MI OWN journal section to write your own thoughts concerning **1, 2, 3,** *allow real life experiences to be your classroom.*

_____

_____

_____

_____

_____

_____

_____

_____

_____

_____

_____

Thought 14

THE EQUATION

Threat the man was infatuated with the lessons of this future world. He did not want to get swallowed in the cycle of an endless Q and A. He was prepared to process pieces of every dimension. Therefore, he picked his final question carefully.

He asked Dr. Hope, "If everything in this world is about the student, what is the meaning behind having a teacher?"

Dr. Hope replied, "The point of a teacher is to increase the perspective of the student. Teachers are intended to insure that every student understands where they are, where they want to go, and how to get there. If any one of these three parts isn't clear within their perspective, teachers help. There are only teachers and students in this world. However, what you choose to learn is always up to you. While individuals continue to learn about this world, they can also teach. Everyone can be a teacher; and everyone can be a student in the process of learning simultaneously. We have to make the decision about where we want to be in the equation."

MI OWN JOURNAL

Use this MI OWN journal section to write your own thoughts concerning **THE EQUATION.** *Are you ready to learn or eager to teach?*

_____

_____

_____

_____

_____

_____

_____

_____

_____

_____

_____

_____

_____

_____

_____

_____

_____

_____

_____

_____

_____

_____

_____

_____

Thought 15
FIND F.U.N.

The man was starting to understand the mind of Dr. Hope. Yet, he wrestled in his mind trying to stabilize the drifting imaginary of a nearly perfect world. He thought to himself, "If the world is only made of teachers and students, then when do people work? How can there be balance between the students of this world and the teachers, especially if everyone is still learning? Without asking aloud, he received an answer.

Dr. Hope said, "The balance between what you want to do and what you need to do is simple – have fun. Fun is the driving force for everybody in both of our dispensations of time. It is why we do everything, with one exception. In your time, some people do things with the expectation of having fun later. It's called the work hard, play hard concept. However, if everyone followed their passions, then work would feel like fun. Fun is a critically important aspect within our dispensation of time. For us, F.U.N. is an acronym. It stands for the Fundamental Understanding of Now. People still work because we pay them too. Making money is fun for everybody. So, in order to make money, people work. Since there is no such thing as a *bad* job, everybody works for the *Fundamental Understanding of Now* (F.U.N.). Unfortunately, in your current dispensation of time, people miss out on Yougwhay because they are only working now to have fun later."

MI OWN JOURNAL

Use this MI OWN journal section to write your own thoughts concerning **FIND FUN.**

Thought 16
THE CONCLUSION
OF THE MATTER

Once F.U.N. was described to the man, he finally realized that he had found the answer he was looking for. He'd traveled alone to a distant dispensation of time to meet his teacher, Dr. Hope. The historian gave the man a sense of balance between his purpose and the meaning of life. He helped him to realize that he had the answer within himself the entire time. Hope was inside his heart before he ever even thought to travel away to this dispensation of time. Without considering his future, he failed to see the simple things that were before his very eyes his entire life. He overlooked the important parts – he needed a teacher – he needed hope. He needed to have F.U.N. – actual fun. Once he realized this, he knew everything he needed to know about this futuristic dispensation, and his own world. So, he thanked the doctor and returned full speed to modern day reality. For the remainder of his life he continued to transition through periods of *good, better, best* by learning to have fun. His time machine was set on a new destination, the man always remained in pursuit of happiness.

MI OWN JOURNAL

Use this MI OWN journal section to write your own thoughts concerning **THE CONCLUSION OF THE MATTER.** *What makes you happy?*

Thought 17
ENDAMILY
The Story That Doesn't Matter

I n the beginning, there was this world. The world was full of beauty and unimaginable natural wonders. However, there was one rule; living creatures could only go around the world eight times before they stopped moving forever. There were two animals in the world that knew this rule quite well. Hence, they strategically devised a plan to move about very carefully. The first animal was named *TuMuch*. She flew around the world faster than anyone. The second animal was named *TuLittle*. He was a small animal with a slim body and a protective shell. His goal wasn't to fill the law quickly but to experience everything the world had to offer in one trip. So, *TuLittle* spent his whole life going slowly around the world until he managed to experience everything. When he finally completed his trip, he was too old to make another journey. *TuMuch,* as swift as she was, also could not repeat her journey. She flew so fast becoming too tired to go around the world a second time.

However, *TuMuch* and *TuLittle* didn't get along at all, even knowing that they were the only two animals on the planet. It is unknown why the two animals didn't get along; no one was there to witness their account. However, *TuMuch* and *TuLittle* wanted to eat each other. But *TuLittle* was too small to eat *TuMuch*; and *TuMuch* couldn't eat *TuLittle* because of his protective shell. Because of this, the only thing that they could think to do was avoid each other forever. So, *TuMuch* forced herself to fly as far away from *TuLittle* as she could. *TuLittle* willed himself to move as far from *TuMuch* as he could. They ended up moving to exact opposite ends of the world.

Since both animals didn't complete their trip, the developing world became bored watching them do nothing for what seemed like eternity. So, on their third rotation around the world, the world itself created another animal; *Patience*. However, he gave this animal a choice to be like anything she wanted to be. The third animal was confused. She knew she didn't want to be like the first animal or the second, because they both never completed their eight trips. However, she knew of no other way. She needed to be unique. As a result, she sought to find balance between flight and being grounded. So *Patience* decided to talk with both of her ancestors in order to understand the best way to go around the world. *Patience* waited for *TuMuch* and *TuLittle* to pass by her as she stood still. As *TuLittle* and *TuMuch* passed by *Patience*, she inquired about their journeys. Eventually, during the seventh trip, the ancestors stopped moving and rested. She called the moments between meeting *TuMuch* and *TuLittle*, time. But after the ancestors stopped moving and time went on, *Patience* began to understand that she had more time on her hands than she could handle alone. The ancestors had left her with questions unanswered. She felt that finding the ancestors would be nearly impossible. If she had wings to fly, she could find *TuMuch,* but might not be able to see *TuLittle.* If she had no legs to slide, then she might be able to see *TuLittle* but would never be close enough to see *TuMuch.* So, she continued to wait for an answer. This caused her more uncertainty. So, the world, understanding her confusion, gifted her with a partner to help her remember the questions and answers. His name was *Timing. Patience* would ask her partner the questions and together they would work to fine the solution. Through their discussion, while waiting, they were able to decide to walk, to run, and to crawl, in order to stay perfectly in the middle of the two spirits. With this knowledge, they would be able to go around the world by running through what didn't matter and crawling toward the things that did. In order not to walk the path more than the law stated, they decided to each start at opposite ends of the world and meet up in the middle. The world, being happy with their idea, made many pairs of animals that each had elements of *TuMuch* and *TuLittle.* The animals helped to assist the others in finding their balanced path. The partners, as they moved around, asked the new animals for direction. They looked for TuMuch and listened for TuLittle – consequently they were lost. However, once they learned to listen more and look further they both found their own way. Once they understood TuMuch and TuLittle to the best of their own ability, they both put themselves right in the middle of the two. They called the path they were making history; and the direction they were going the future. They walked back and forth through their own created paths until they finally found what they were looking for – they found one another. Once the animals finished their first journey with balance, the world allowed them to multiply their numbers and forge new paths together. Once they had children, they set out to discover more.

However, the children of the two balanced parents were twins who decided to make a better path on their own. The parents also chose to start a new exploration. They walked a new path together, searching for the resting place of their ancestors. After every animal found their own path in life, the world was finally finished.

MI OWN JOURNAL

Use this MI OWN journal section to write your own thoughts concerning **ENDAMILY,** *The Story that Doesn't Matter. Is there an antagonist in your life? What would your life story look like without the antagonist? Why do you think your life would be better without the antagonist?*

_____

_____

_____

Section II
MI OWN CHOICES

Choice 1
Criminal Minds, *Part I*

Hey Mr. Officer!

Officer: Oh! Hey Bill, where are you off to?

Bill: Just going to sit around making six figures, profiting off slave labor in China and American migrant workers.

Officer: Migrants! Those lazy sons of guns. I hate those guys.

Bill: Me too, Dave, me too. That's why we keep our office minority free.

Officer: That's good to hear, Bill. I'm on my way to arrest the minorities you won't hire for trying to make money in the only way they've come to know how. Depending on where the day takes me, or I might just harass innocent minorities.

Bill: That sure sounds swell, Dave. Well you have fun with that.

Officer: You too, Bill, I'll see you later.

MI OWN JOURNAL

Use this MI OWN journal section to write your own thoughts concerning **CRIMNAL MINDS.** *How do ethical dilemmas define your choices?*

_____
_____
_____
_____
_____
_____

Choice 2
Criminal Minds, *Part II*

Hey Bill, how was work?

Bill: It was great. Oh, boy, did we kick the environments keister today.

Officer: That's good too hear, Bill. How was your weekend, by the way?

Bill: It was pretty crazy, Dave. I got into a drunken scuffle at a bar down the way. I ended up killing the guy.

Officer: Wow! Billy, it's a good thing you weren't high.

Bill: Yeah definitely, luckily, he was a minority. So, it was obviously in self-defense.

Officer: Obviously. (As he winks his eye). Of course… God, I hate minorities. They are a danger to our society. Who knows when they'll hurt someone next. You know what, I'm going to go shoot one right now just to keep us safe.

Bill: What a good idea! Take my gun, you can plant it on him later.

Officer: Thanks Billy, but no need. I'll just tell him to pull out his wallet, and then say he was reaching for a weapon.

Bill: Golly Dave, you sure are something else. Well you have fun with that. I'm going to go home and teach my children my superior ideologies. Hopefully they'll feel unsafe around minorities by the time they're 10-years-old.

Officer: You're a good man bill. Have a nice rest of

your day.

MI OWN JOURNAL

Use this MI OWN journal section to write your own thoughts concerning **CRIMINAL MINDS,** *experiencing good without bad. Do you ever use hate to feel safe? Why do people allow hatred to dictate their choices, and do you?*

_____

_____

_____

_____

_____

_____

_____

_____

_____

_____

_____

_____

_____

_____

_____

_____

_____

_____

_____

_____

Choice 3
Criminal Minds, *Part III*

Hey Mr. officer!

Officer: Hey Bill what are you doing out here?

Bill: Oh, just grabbing a late meal for the wife and I. Funny story. As I driving to pick up some food, I saw three minorities on the corner. And after I locked my windows, I chuckled a little, because I realized that statistically speaking at least one of them will see jail time before they die.

Officer: Ha ha ha! That is a hoot, but do you want to hear something that will knock your socks off? I drove past that corner before I saw you. I just finished arresting one off those three.

Bill: Ha ha ha! Isn't that comedic. What did he do?

Officer: Nothing. He looked suspicious. So, I said he pulled a gun on me. Luckily, he's poor. Now that scoundrel will be locked up and off the streets for good. I'm sure *those people* won't be able to afford bail. So, one of them default-lawyers, who'll get three minutes to review his case, will probably convince him to take a plead guilty. Not to mention, when on parole as a felon no one will hire him. How about that, Bill!

Bill: That's great, Dave. Thanks for keeping us safe. I'd rather see a thousand innocent minorities get locked up then see one guilty man walk free.

Officer: And that's what we do Bill. That's what we do. Have a good night.

MI OWN JOURNAL

Use this MI OWN journal section to write your own thoughts concerning **CRIMINAL MINDS.** *Have you ever been faced with a moral dilemma? Why do you think your enemies are bad?*

Choice 4
Ordinary
Jokes of a Writer

Love is just like hair- if too much of it gets in your eyes, you can't see clearly.

The life of the man on the boat who finally makes it to the harbor; and has learned to swim only after he found land.

A man who studies everything he could in the world just to remember that there was never a test to take.

A recreated story of the first door ever.

A man who tries to understand his whole life until he realizes that he can just look in a mirror to understand himself.

A man who forgot to say thank you because he was so proud of himself.

A man who studies for a test he never even has to take only to realize that he wasn't enrolled in school anymore anyway.

A boy who gets sick of candy because his mom works at a candy store.

A dog that only barks when spoken to because he thinks he's talking.

A coward that loves to be dangerous. A danger that is scared of everything. A hero whose super power is crying.

A robot who can only understand himself through the eyes of others.

The late man, the early man.

Talk about this and that. I need to be balanced.

A man with no voice who wanted to talk.

A man who is afraid of water until he realizes he is ice.

A man who hates money, because he wants to be rich.

A man who only talked to babies, because he didn't want to put up with people's poo.

A boy who cried wolf because he was scared of sheep.

A sheep that ate with wolves to feel safer.

Food that only wanted to eat itself.

People that live alone because they only want to hear themselves talk.

A man scared of pooping.

A woman scared of breast.

Cows scared of milk.

Ice scared of beating up water.

A man that shoots anyone afraid of cops.

A person that is scared of people because they have shadows.

A boy that didn't want to sleep because he forgot how.

The problem with mental health is also the solution to every problem on earth; people think they are different. It makes people afraid of ice when everyone is made of water.

A normal man that wants to be extra ordinary.

Jokes of a Historian

I gave a name to others in time but I never named myself. I chose to be Doctor Hope.

The new beginning - written for Mi Own mental health.

MI OWN JOURNAL

Use this MI OWN journal section to write your own thoughts concerning **ORDINARY,** *Jokes of a Writer. Why do some people take life too seriously? Is it okay to have fun throughout difficult situations? How important is laughter to you? How do you have fun during challenging times?*

_____

_____

_____

_____

_____

_____

_____

_____

_____

_____

_____

_____

_____

_____

_____

_____

_____

_____

_____

_____

_____

Choice 5
Endamily
I'm Home

There is a creation story about two sons of *Patience* and *Timing*; they were two perfectly balanced animals. One son lived on a planet called *Hot,* and the other lived on a planet called *Cold.* Each planet was unique, but different. They each created their own planets. After walking the path of life throughout the whole world they each decided to create their own space of adventure. Planet Hot created confidence and planet Cold created hope. However, they each wanted to be on each other's planet, because they were brothers who loved one another. So, every year they would bring all the best stuff from their planets and eat together on the planet of their parents. They called the space where they ate, *Faith.* They had a huge feast and relished their time together. This feast would get better each year, because the brothers kept growing and making new foods after learning more about each other's recipes. The recipes were called *facts* and *emotions.* Finally, the last two recipes created was so similar that they laughed upon seeing the results. One dish was called *man and* the other was called *woman.* When the sons had dinner with man and woman it was lots of fun. It was so much fun that they never ate the man and woman. Afterward, every year following, *man* and *woman* came over with the sons. Eventually the sons stopped eating all the meals and began to teach *man* and *woman* how to cook for themselves. All the meals were completely good, but the sons never ate them entirely, because they were such a delight to have around. Eventually, *man* and *woman* began to make their own foods that would stay on the middle planet between Hot and Cold. They were always warmer or cooler than the last mixture, but each creation was always perfect.

MI OWN JOURNAL

Use this MI OWN journal section to write your own thoughts concerning **ENDAMILY,** *I'm home. Who do you enjoy being around, and why?*

_____

_____

_____

_____

_____

_____

_____

_____

_____

_____

_____

_____

_____

_____

_____

_____

_____

_____

Choice 6
THE SEARCH FOR PERFECT
The Emotional Genius

The emotional family man always seeks perfection. What happens to the writer after he comes back to his present time? He discovers that his trip was all for nothing, except it was fun. He gets stuck in a river that he calls time. The man names the river time because he believes that he is stuck in a river that is flowing backwards in time. Throughout his euphoric experience he thought he was going back in time. However, in reality, the man was only stuck in one small section of a large river. The river was named time, but he had no clue that he wasn't moving along the current of the river. The man was not moving because the river was not flowing within the small section. He was actually stuck in a portion of the river, surrounded by rocks. He sees the rocks through the window of the time machine; he also sees bubbles coming from the river. He doesn't understand why he can only see rocks and bubbles. As a result, he makes an assumption that they are cosmic entities stuck between time.

He believes that the time machine has him trapped between the past and the future. He then begins to feel as though he has been transformed. He sees himself as a mix between a rock and a bubble. He suddenly becomes afraid of what his transformation will look like. This inward battle spiraled from his own thoughts and perspectives. He is in a rapidly moving river that is not flowing in the spot where he is located. He is stuck between two massive mountain-like landscapes. Eventually, he believes he is a rock. He sees bubbles above him, so he believes that he might also be a bubble. His diluted perspective has transformed him into something he is afraid to look at. In reality, the only thing that could fix his perspective is a mirror, but he refuses to look. He was scared of himself.

He got scared enough to the point that he tried to change his perspective by only looking down at the rocks; not the bubbles. however; this then led him to believe that he was stuck in time between two giant collections of lifeless rocks. His delusional state caused him to start believing he was useless, worthless, unnecessary and without meaning. He believed in the dead rock concept so much that he started to believe that he himself had turned into one. Luckily, every time he looked around he was reminded that he could move, and remembered that he had moved before. The man would move around again and again within the time machine in order to remember that he was a man. He no longer felt like a rock after he moved around. He did feel like a rock whenever he looked through the window. It scared him to remember that he might be trapped in time, but he was not. He was just not in a spot where the river could reach him. He had to get out of that difficult and bad place.

Unfortunately, he failed to realize that he was in a bad place. He was overwhelmingly excited to occupy his own space in time. His adrenalin sparked a sense of eagerness for the future. This excitement forced him to fail at basic life skills – he overlooked eating and sleeping. He did nothing he was physically capable of achieving. All he did was write books full of questions. He rewrote the questions that he had asked Doctor Hope. He repeated the questions, in order to remember. Although, he kept forgetting to write down the answers. He soon grew impatient, wanting to speed up the flow of the river. As a result, he spent all his time neglecting his body, trying everything to make the time machine in the river go faster. He refused to acknowledge that he was going crazy, like a mad scientist. He believed that his own emotions didn't exist anymore. He was trying to remember all the answers while attempting to accelerate time. Due to this, he started to lose track of things – nothing registered that he aimed to initially recall. Unfortunately, failure started causing him to go mad.

He only wanted to change the time he came from, in order to create a better one. However, he never realized that the river was unchangeable. It only flows in one direction. The man refused to understand the scientific equations that caused the river to flow in that certain direction. He was unable to look around and see the small section he was stuck in.

So, even though he was extremely tired and hungry, he never left his dark room. He desperately tried to observe reality from the confinement of his time machine - without food, sleep or relaxation – the mental experience was intense. His only focus was changing his past, but he began to fear the time he came from. He never acknowledged his fear. He was confident that his emotions wouldn't exist in a better time. So, he continues to let himself go mad and fear the world. Finally, he started to become so scared of the world that he came from that he desired to go back to Doctor Hope. He felt he needed to understand the doctor more, in effort to live without fear. Unfortunately, the man didn't realize what his own fear was. He was afraid of being different than the man he set out to become. He wanted to be more like Dr. Hope, but he needed to ask more questions. He hoped that answers would help him relax. In order to search for Doctor Hope, he decided it was time to change his view. It seemed like nearly a decade passed by the time he left his room. Upon escaping from his room of isolation, he saw light. Light had become distant and foreign. He realized he'd been living in darkness during the entire experience. His eyes had become strained from focusing too hard within the darkness.

He grabbed his glasses and slowly came of out of the time machine. He sat on top of it as though it were a raft for safety. At the moment he was able to see over the rocks. Immediately, he realizes that he was just stuck in a small section – not stuck in time. So, he moved the rocks and the machine began to flow again. This new perspective allowed him to be certain that he could move whenever he wanted. He started enjoying the time he had in the river. He wrote stories that were fun to write and books that made him feel like he wasn't stuck anymore. His thoughts felt clear. Once he had clear thoughts, he started seeing people on the shores of the river. He would talk to these people as they went by – telling them about the fun that the future world held for them. He wrote their questions and found creative ways to answer them using a *Mi Own Collection* of thoughts. Eventually, he had so much information about the future world that he began to feel hopeful about his own life. He saw the future through clear lenses.

Once he re-enters the imperfect time machine, he sees water everywhere. At first sight, he was tremendously scared. He couldn't help but to think he was going to drown, before realizing there was only a leak in the time machine. He found the leak, which made him laugh. This was the first laughter he felt in a long time – he released a decade of joy. At that comical moment, he had a euphoric epiphany that though he named the river after the time machine, he should've named the time machine after the river. The river has no holes; the time machine does. Afterward, he made a joke. His entire perspective changes. He desires to stop making a fuss over remembering all the answers. He then starts to acknowledge that everybody makes mistakes – there will always be holes in the past, the present and the future. Even the perfect world has imperfections.

He understands why he never can go back in time. The answer was simple, yet complex: we must all keep moving forward – despite life's difficulties, we must advance through time. His time machine had been broken during his entire experience with the darkness. Yet, the river was real. When he stepped out of the time machine he absorbed as much of the light as possible. The light empowered him to read the questions clearly in order to find fixes and answers. Instead of fixing the questions in the book, he decides to create a book of answers. While sitting on top of the time machine writing, he sees people floating down the river alone. Although he enjoyed writing the book more than anything, he realized it was consuming him. Through conversations with others, he realized he wasn't taking care of his body. So, he used the water in the time machine to wash up. As soon as he started to tend to his personal needs, the time machine stopped moving. In fact, the river came to an end. The time machine officially served its final purpose. He leaves the time machine and goes outside. The river came to an end next to a gate. The gate, wide open, stood before a clear field.

The grass in this field was greener than any grass he'd ever seen. He was excited to go into the clear field to start his new adventure. Before he went in, he saw a sign. The sign before the gate said; "Future trash heap". After reading the sign he laughed harder than ever. Seeing the sign made him happier than anything in a long while. The man was happy. He was so happy that he destroyed the time machine. He was so happy that he threw it into the future trash heap. As he stood inside the clear field, he cried. He was truly happy to start his next adventure. So, he cried tears of joy. He was confused and emotional; but he was truly happy. So, he decided that he would search again for Doctor Hope. Not to ask more questions, but to laugh with him. He wanted to thank the doctor. He realized that the doctor hadn't just given him hope, but medicine. Laughter was his medicine. Dr. Hope gave the man the medicine he needed most, which was fun. Now the man wanted to have fun forever. He had no idea what time he was in, because the time machine had been destroyed. Yet, he knew that no matter where he was, he'd have *the time of his life.*

MI OWN JOURNAL

Use this MI OWN journal section to write your own thoughts concerning **THE SEARCH FOR PERFECT** – *make it fun!*

Choice 7

HOMELESS

Unsolved Thoughts of a Writer

Things Change Quickly:

Enjoy what you can before you can't.

The Frame:

Art can speak a thousand words, while songs beautify a few. Yet no art could sing to me the words I feel from you.

Wanting More Leads to Nothing:

Greed is the evil twin of ambition. Fueled by material possession, it is a wild fire that ravages the mind.

We Spend Our Lives Dying:

A fruit fly's lifespan is 3-14 days. Is that enough time to live? Sea turtles live for centuries; but at the end of their life, is it still incomplete?

Spring Cleaning:

You can't hold on to everything.

Time is Slow:

Time changes things, but things hardly every change.

Violence:

Violence is a causation of violence without relation to the causation of violence, initially.

New Mirror:

Think like the person you want to become.

Good Spending Habits:

The only true currency is time. I would give away $100,000 now, if it only took 3 seconds to make up.

What is a Family:

What is a father, if he acts like a big brother? What is a mother, if she doesn't care for you? What is a cousin, if y'all have never met?

Throw the Baby Out:

The funny thing about hell is that it is for eternity. That means that "God" punishes you for an infinite amount of time for what you did in an infinitely small percentage of that time. That's like my father spanking me for my entire life, because I kicked him as a baby.

Blood Stains:

If a person was put into a different environment, would he still end of in the same path he is in life now.

The Oxymoron:

What does it mean to act black? Being black shouldn't mean acting loud, aggressive, and without a filter. Just like acting white shouldn't mean being intelligent or privileged. When we accept ignorance as our identity, we become part of the problem.

The Mirror:

If people are all the same, then hate is self-reflection. If people are all the same then, love is self-reflection. If people are all the same then to not believe in the hearts of others, to deny, is self-rejection.

Maybe Later:

Don't put things aside. When you say you will do it when you're not busy, you're planning for a time that will never come. If you are alive, there will always be stuff to do. You must make time for the things that will make you better and do them regardless of your circumstance.

Sharing is Caring:

If you don't share, people will steal. However, stealing and sharing are incompatible. Stealing cannot exist with sharing. This means it is smarter to work towards sharing then against stealing; because sharing is better. Sharing helps you reach goals much quicker, than if you were to try things on your own.

The Modern-day Nobody:

I don't believe I am the modern day anybody. I believe in myself.

I am not chasing anybody else's accomplishments. I believe in myself. I know I can never be someone else, and I like that idea; no one else will ever be me. I believe in myself.

I Think So Maybe:

The reason that religions took so long to disprove is because people thought that since it is so confusing it must be true. The reason people thought that science was wrong is because it was so simple that it must be untrue. To the ill-informed, confusion can lead to certainty.

Is There Life Out There:

Imagine I'm holding a big box. Is there a cat in the box? You can't see what's in the box. You can guess what it is based on the diameter of the box or the shape of the box. You can even hear it purr. But you can't ever know if it was truly a cat until you see it. That didn't answer your question. It led to a bigger question of, does it matter? Keep asking questions and eventually you will understand everything. Because the key to understanding is discovering the bigger question.

Red Cabbage:

Why is a red cabbage called a red cabbage when it is obviously purple? How did it get its name? Maybe whoever named it saw red instead of purple. It's possible that everybody sees the same color a different way. One man's orange can be another man's blue, but still be called orange for both. The perspective of another person can never be completely seen by someone else; and each person's view of the world can never be determined by others. We are completely unique. Even still, if the entity that named red cabbage had a view of purple that was my view of red, he would still call it purple. So why did he call it red?

Why Not:

It would be odd to see, on a city street or on a museum, people dancing; twerking and grinding on each other publicly. Yet, unequivocally by nature, those are among the things that we want to do. For some reason, we banish those deep desires and hide them under a cloak of sophistication. Why do we live unfulfilling lives for the sake of civility? Money, fame and power are all examples of the tools now necessary to have the freedom to enjoy life's pleasures. As a result, they are perceived as our desires. When in reality, our wants are so basic they could be achieved easily. Why have we, as a society, over complicated our ambitions and extruded the routes in which to achieve them. Are we in denial of our motivations, because we cling to the incorrect perception that they are superior to that of an animal? Society has become a prison, baring us away from a life enjoyed simplistically.

Laughing, but Serious:

I used to be afraid of Jabba the hut. When he sets a trap for princess Leya in the 6th Star Wars, he makes a loud maniacal laugh as he reveals himself to the princess. That laugh senselessly scared me as a kid. My dad noticed this and began to mock Jabba's laugh. It scared me so much that I would run and hide. He chased me around making that laugh whenever he knew where I was hiding. It became a game. It was fun. I enjoyed playing with my father. Now, every time I hear Jabba's laugh, I reminisce happily over those moments. He turned my fear into my fondest childhood memories. Crazy how emotions for the same thing can change so drastically.

New Change

As we sat in the kitchen, and my mom spoke on-and-on about how it was no ones' fault and how they still love us, I remembered a time where we were all happy. In that very kitchen we used to enjoy, we used to feel joy, on every occasion that we were together. Mom would cook something that always had such an inviting aroma. My brother would sit at the table doing homework, and my dad would walk in, all dressed up and formal, and shout, "Hello" to everyone. Then we, the family, would tell stories about our day, and joke, and laugh as if we were at the best place on earth. One day, in that same kitchen, she said the word divorce, and I was brought back to my new reality. I was back in this place that was no longer the kitchen I once knew. I was now surrounded by people that didn't make one another happy anymore. I felt an odd emotion then. It was difficult to find an accurate word for such a feeling. I was sad, but I didn't feel sadness. I was hurt, but I was not feeling pain. This emotion, when it had finally been pinpointed, was a different feeling then the ones I thought I was supposed to have. I guess there's no rule book for this, and many other indescribable disappointments. I felt nostalgia. I couldn't help but miss those moments we loved together. I couldn't help but loath change for taking the family I once knew. I felt hopeless – how could I live a different or better life than the parents I so esteemed throughout my childhood. Probably, for the first time, I felt regret. Why? When we were happy or in this kitchen as a family, why didn't I cherish those moments. Why didn't I look around and just admire what we shared? If only I hadn't been so concerned with the status of the meal – wondering when we could eat. I remember trying to figure out how to sneak a quick sample. Now, I'm left with the ultimate emptiness; trapped in the ghost of a room with people that don't make each other happy anymore.

There's Too Much in Life to Live for:

Life's a beach, but it's hard to see the joy in life with shades on.

You Won't Be Remembered:

The people you say goodbye to, die too. Boo-hoo. Who's there to cry to? You die, who knew? You lived, says who?

The Future Never Comes:

*W*asted *A*mbition, *I*mperfect *T*iming, *I*mplementing *N*othing. *G*iving_*F*ormer *O*pportunities *R*eason_*T*o *M*ove *O*nward. *R*elentlessly *R*eflecting *O*nly *W*hen_*A*bsolute *N*othingness *D*uels *W*ithin. *A*ll *S*urreal *T*houghts *I*rrevocably *N*ever *G*ot_*T*o *O*utshine *D*ull *A*ctions. *Y*olo **(Waiting for Tomorrow and Wasting Today)** This seems like Pointless Misfortune. Why wish my brother harm? We are all prisoners of this world, generated to be pitiful servants to some cruel god, or evermore imaginable, some meaningless mishap of involuntary creation. We are all cursed to waste away in this strange place. So, why wish my brother harm simply because he is slightly more or less lucky than me?

The Smartest Dummy

I'm too dumb to love again, but too smart to hate. I'm too wise to know the joys of life. I'm too dumb to relate. I'm too dumb to realize that life is good. I'm too smart to trust in fate. I'm the wisest fool I'll ever know and it's such a sorry state.

101

I'm Stuck On a Boat:

Time flows like a river. I am trapped in the current. The joys of life lie peacefully on the shore, but I pass them by as time pushes forward. Time never quickens, never slows, yet I feel it is moving too fast. I can't push against the tide; I can't anchor down. I can only move forward, whether I want to or not. I have no idea where the river will pass. I can't predict the storms yet to come. I can't predict the beauty left to see. I only know the destination. I am headed toward a waterfall.

Connected to Nothing:

The big apple is the new big brother. He is *sat* in the universe like a *light*. He's positioned in the galaxy facing the world dictating, influencing and controlling the masses. It's crazy how he's taken over so impressively. Tele screens must have cocaine in the recipe. We don't need a terabyte or megabyte to see that the big apple took a big bite from humanity. There are books about ancient lives lived happily, distant from electricity. Silly me, I can't talk about being free. Because if I do, I'll be called a hypocrite then beaten virtually. The screens imprisoned everyone and locked you up along with me. That's why I don't have a plea. Because I can't speak about breaking out, I don't know how without a key, even then my battery is dead. A world united by the satellite somehow becoming increasingly separated. A social virus is affecting a whole generation – and it is deadly. We give power to the things that somehow empower us. Why is it when our devices die we feel powerless?

Party Animals:

I've observed that human nature can be exposed at a party. Reason being, there is an excuse to reveal it. Without thought, people are basic creatures driven by primal instinct. Correspondently, thought is unwanted at parties, hence the desire for mind numbing drugs. This makes parties nothing more than a gathering ground for simple beast. The use of dark lights and deafening noise, in fact, can be seen as an attempt to further expose beastly instinct. They prey on our natural response toward those stimulants. Free from the constraints of civility, humans have basic tendencies. Girls act cute and guys act cool. Then begins a mating ritual, parallel in weirdness to any other found in nature. Girls shake their booty to attract the opposite sex. In response a male will try to grind on the back of the dancing woman. If the girl accepts him as a mate, then she will continue. This phenomenon has been named twerking. It is only one example of our odd behavior as party animals.

MI OWN JOURNAL

Use this MI OWN journal section to write your own thoughts concerning **HOMELESS,** words will give new meaning to empty spaces in your life. Think about it and write it.

Time Machine

Section III
MI OWN EMOTIONS

Emotion 1
PAIN PERSISTS
HOMELESS: Short Story

I feel pain. Everyday I go to school and get beat by the people around me, my friends. I'm getting beat everyday, without getting a chance to heal. I'm getting beat everyday and I can't take much more pain, the torture is hurting tremendously. I go home, and I beat my brother. Maybe that will distract me from *Mi Own* pain. I hurt my brother because I am hurting. Unfortunately, my brother can't handle *Mi Own* pain either. How can he escape the pain he feels? What if there's no distraction for him? He can't heal either. My brother feels pain. Everyday He goes home and gets beat by the people around him. He's getting beat everyday and he can't take much more.

Finally, he tells me: "I'm hurting, and you're the one hurting me. I don't want to hurt anymore." He tells me he's going to kill himself, because he can't take the pain. I understand. I understand, because I'm hurting, too. I can't handle *Mi Own* pain either. I understand. I replied, "Don't die, maybe we can handle our pain together. I don't want to hurt you. I don't want to give you *Mi Own* pain anymore. I don't want to hurt like this anymore. Together we can find a way to not hurt."

MI OWN JOURNAL

Use this MI OWN journal section to write your own thoughts concerning **PAIN PERSISTS.**

_____

_____

_____

_____

_____

_____

_____

_____

_____

_____

_____

_____

_____

_____

_____

_____

_____

_____

_____

_____

_____

_____

_____

_____

_____

_____

_____

_____

Emotion 2

IT IS BETTER UNDERGROUND

HOMELESS: SHORT STORY

A very long time from now, in a nearby galaxy there lived the devil. The devil was the king of the underworld. This place was a dark fiery abyss of lost soul and sadness. As the king of such a place, the devil was always considered hateful. He was called an evil trickster who only found enjoyment by being bad. He was indeed all those things of course, but he began to wonder what was so wrong with the way he lived. He liked his kingdom of fire and brimstone. It was his castle, his home, and he enjoyed living there. He liked his demeanor, the way he wasn't controlled by anyone or anything. He had the power to take anything he desired, maybe it was through trickery and deception, but isn't that how most people succeed anyway? So, what was so wrong about him, he wondered. Why was he so looked down upon? So, as he pondered these questions, he decided that he would go on a quest to find knowledge. He wanted to discover why people assumed life is so much better when they practice kindness, generosity and good will toward people. To do this, he left his humble abode and traveled to the world above ground. There he became surrounded by weird and annoying people living meaningless and unhappy lives. He found the world above disgusting, but to complete his quest for knowledge, he ignored his feelings and proceeded on his quest to be nice and generous to everyone he encountered. Oddly, the devil soon realized that the nicer he was, the more people took advantage of him. All of the so-called friends that he made from his attitude adjustment, only misused him for the gifts he could provide. People took his kindness for weakness and then proceeded to walk over him. He was always surrounded by fake friends. Yet he found himself feeling more alone than when he was in hell. Still, the devil felt that there had to be some sort of benefit to being good. So, he decided to continue his investigation. He wandered upon a pure and innocent man and sent him on a quest to save a damsel in distress from a life of prostitution and dirtiness. The devil watched as the pure man fell head over heels for the girl and proceeded to give her all the love and resources available to please her. He cared for her, supported her, catered to her and paid her way on every occasion. He loved that girl. Yet the devil began to discover something within the damsel that he did not like. The devil saw too much of himself in that girl, the parts that even he despised.

The alleged good-hearted devil watched in dismay as the girl drained the poor boy. She took up all his time, his money and his happiness. She controlled him. She took advantage of him. The damsel enjoyed watching him faun over her. She craved his attention and grew more powerful from his affection. Yet, the more love that the pure boy displayed, the less the girl appreciated it. Eventually, she became bored of the boy and left him.

The pure boy became lost in depression. Having given his whole heart to that temptress, the boy now felt empty and sad. The pure boy cried out to God, whom the devil was not fond of, and asked, "Why God? Why must good men hurt so bad?" Nevertheless, the devil heard his plea, and wondered the same. After that gloomy endeavor, the devil decided that his quest was complete. He discovered that kindness got him nowhere in life. It only attracted fake friends and people looking to take advantage of the kindness he displayed. Love and compassion leads to heartbreak and depression. Throughout it all, he found that he was happier alone in the hot discomfort of hell, tricking others to get what he wanted, and choosing to hate instead of love. He had learned everything he needed to know about the other world and decided that it was better underground.

MI OWN JOURNAL

Use this MI OWN journal section to write your own thoughts concerning **IT IS BETTER UNDERGROUND.** *Why do people take kindness for weakness?*

_____

_____

_____

Emotion 3
WATCH YOUR MOUTH
HOMELESS SHORT STORY

Hello out there, my name is Barbra Owens, and I'm here with a young upcoming extraordinaire named *Yu*, the man. I'm sure you've heard of him by now and we are elated to have him here on the show today. "Thank you Barbra, he said. "I'm happy to be here."

"Let's get right into this interview. Recently there was a man claiming that children should be taught to swear or use profanity as a part of their English vocabulary. What are your thoughts on the issue," Barbra asked?

Yu responded, "That is a good question Barbra. I believe that emotional control defines difference between professional and personal relationships. Showing emotions make you relatable, but diminishes professionalism in return. People often swear to convey strong and passionate emotion. It allows them to display a feeling of being able to relate. Right now, you're smiling at me to relate to the TV audience by showing them you're happy. That makes this conversation seem less professional and more fun to watch. If we were to look into the Oval Office during a cabinet meeting, you would probably see straight stern faces conversing while trying to seem as professional as possible. Being able to relate can be very useful, but overuse can be a danger. Although you want to be relatable to the TV audience, you would never cuss at me, even if I said something outlandish or disagreeable. If you did, it would show too much emotion and perhaps tarnish your professional appearance. It would lessen the intellectual value of all your prior statements. It might even make the whole show seem like an unreliable source for serious information. With that being said, I would punish my children if they ever swore around me, not because I think cursing is evil, but because it teaches them emotional control when communicating."

MI OWN JOURNAL

Use this MI OWN journal section to write your own thoughts concerning **WATCH YOUR MOUTH.** *What do you consider to be proper language?*

Emotion 4
NEVER EAT
HOMELESS: SHORT STORY

I n the wild, when you're hungry, or hoping to avoid dropping dead from malnourishment, you hunt as though your life depends on it. At that point, it does. The same philosophy can be applied to money, especially when you're broke. Poor people are known to hustle like there's no other way to live. Unfortunately, people don't think about what happens when they catch the prey. Once they catch the meal, they grow comfortable. They eat off it and find new ways to make it last longer or taste better. They munch as though the supply will never run out. In modern times, people do the same. They chase one idea that will bring wealth and then slightly improve it forever. However, the pure hunter never eats. The pure hunter takes the little scrapes from his kill, no matter how big, and barely survives as he goes out to strike again. As a result, the pure hunter is more successful and will have more meat than any other hunter in the wild. This is because the hunter has an endless supply of a different assortment of meat. Yet, the hunter still never eats. Here's why? The pure hunter would rather chase happiness than be happy. He would rather achieve every goal, and make more goals, rather than rest and sleep happily. According to the pure hunter, as blissful as it may be and as joyous as it may feel, sleep is death. Death is the end of your dreams, death is the end of the possibility of more. Even if you catch your prey, and then live a happy life for 100 years reaping the rewards, you've died already. This is because your life ended with that hunt. No matter how tasty your current prey is, you will never know how extraordinary your next prey could have been.

People say you need to work hard to be happy. You don't. You can sit around on the couch all day and be the happiest man alive. However, you need to work hard to reach your goals. The purpose of life is to strive for more, because if you don't, it's as if you're already dead.

The Problem:

The problem with the never eat story is that it idolizes the hunter. He has a purpose, but the reward means nothing to him. What is the point of hunting when you don't eat? What is the meaning behind his hunt?

Note to Self

Hey future me. I hope you feel better than you used to be.
I hope you're happier than I am usually.
I hope you see life more beautifully.
I hope you're not blinded by misery.
I hope you think of life as a sight to see. I hope you have
finally said goodbye to me.

MI OWN JOURNAL

Use this MI OWN journal section to write your own thoughts concerning **NEVER EAT.**

Section IV
MI OWN DECISIONS

Decision 1
YU Make
*Freedom, Fun, Perfection
and Organization*

The first decision is to learn more. The second decision is to speak and listen. The third decision is to have confidence, faith and hope. The final decision is to be ordinary and unique. In order to make decisions, you must first learn how to prioritize your choices.

The first choice is always to think first. The last choice is to categorize your choices or options. For example, you must start with a question in order to seek answers. Where we start in our thought processes is often the same place we will end. Consider your emotions.

The same emotions we feel before we discover our choices and make decisions, are often the same emotions we experience afterward. When we make decisions, we must remember how they will impact, affect, build up or destroy those around us. We are all connected through water, yet unique because we are not the same. *Mi Own* time throughout this entire book, no matter how long it takes to read it, whether hours for some and days for others. Everyone must be allowed space and time to be an individual, while realizing they are part of a greater majority. A mirror will reflect a different image for everyone, but the mirror never changes. We will all experience *Mi Own* thoughts, emotions, choices and decisions, and they will determine the outcome of our lives. There is a serenity prayer that states:

"God, grant me the serenity to accept the things I cannot change, courage to change the things I can, and wisdom to know the difference." - **by Reinhold Niebuhr**

Without this framework of thinking when making decisions, we will find ourselves making emotional decisions that will leave us stuck in the same small sections and pitfalls of life.

Emotions change. Art will inspire emotions when we see it; music stimulates when we hear it, food fuels when we taste it, and so on. However, inspiration is not the key to perfection – we will always make mistakes, feel emotional and gain new inspirations. We only need ears, eyes and senses to open our first door, and continue transitioning to new dimensions thereafter. Avoid getting trapped by changing emotions. You need faith to know what's on the other side. Faith is not based on temporal or changing emotions. Faith is the ability to open doors without external stimulates – it is the substance that Doctor Hope offers. Faith allows us to breath, relax and let go. When we are broken by negative thoughts, erratic emotions, changing choices and difficult decisions, hope will equip us to sleep well and live healthy.

MI OWN JOURNAL

Use this MI OWN journal section to write your own thoughts concerning **DECISIONS** *Yu Make.*

_____

_____

_____

_____

_____

_____

_____

_____

_____

_____

_____

_____

_____

_____

_____

_____

_____

_____

_____

_____

_____

_____

_____

_____

Decision 2
My Understanding
The Humble Prideful Oxymoron

Who am I. I am a re-definition of me, myself and I. I make mistakes, but I forgive myself. I have to live above guilt, fear and self-defeat, if I want to be a better me. Afterward, I can be greater than my old self. Who I am, and who you view yourself as, determines whether or not the end will even matter to you.

This section of The Mi Own Collection is specifically dedicated to my brother – there is a truth for every joke, I chose to hear the jokes. The funny thing about mental health is that you never know what mental issues you have until someone else tells you.

I CONQUERED ANXIETY

Everyone gets nervous. Even the man who has done everything would be a little scared to try it again. My solution to anxiety was to ignore it. I would do the things that scared me the most, just so I wouldn't be scared to do them anymore. No matter how often you do things, you can never get rid of fear. I didn't accept this reality as fact. However, I ended up hurting myself, mentally. Sometimes fear is there to protect us from our own fearless nature. I refused to listen to my common sense and experienced negative results.

I STOOD FACE-TO-FACE WITH DEPRESSION

No matter how happy you claim to be; No matter how happy you truly are; No matter how much happiness you feel; everyone experiences sadness sometimes. It's a part of human nature to feel things that we sometimes don't want to, but it never last forever. I forgot that sadness comes and goes and started to fear that it would stay forever.

I MANAGED STRESS

I was in a new situation. New situations are always stressful. I was putting pressure on myself to figure it out on my own. One person will never have all the answers in life. I had to learn to accept that on my own, I can't do it all.

I EMBRACED SLEEP

I thought that sleep was a waste of time. I was so focused on being perfect that I didn't think that I needed sleep at all. I took short naps throughout the day in order to have energy to keep working for hours, but I ended up not sleeping completely, for more than two weeks. People need sleep. I forgot that simple fact and had to relearn the hard way.

WHAT I LEARNED AFTER

I recently learned so much about myself. I learned that I have emotions and that I make mistakes. Most importantly, I learned to forgive myself and keep trying to get better. I learned that I can be the best me on the planet, because I have no competition.

LOOKING FORWARD

The scariest aspect of mental health challenges is also the solution to every problem that has ever been solved. The same thing that makes us unique is what makes us spectacular. If we were all the same, nothing new would ever be created. That's what makes people perfect.

RE-EXPLANATION

I never believed in mental health. I always thought that a man could do anything he set his mind to do. The mind controls everything, but it needs to be taken care of just as much as any other physical part of the body. Mental health is a real issue. I wrote this book as I desperately aimed to restore *Mi Own* (my own) mental health. While writing, I realized that everyone struggles with seasons of mental health. My solution was to write an abstract book that could recreate memories and capture a sense of hope for readers. Ultimately, the solution seems simple; sleep well, eat well, and let your mind rest. Sometimes, simplicity is complex.

RE-EXPLANATION II

The worst thing I've ever done is lie to myself. I had to learn about myself in the most uncomfortable way possible. Unfortunately, for me, I was put into a situation where l had to face my biggest fears one giant at a time. People face fears every day. Although, I had to face them when I became most afraid. I soon learned that I'd had more fears than I'd realized. After evaluating my fears one-by-one, I soon learned that most people I've encountered share similar thoughts. My biggest fear was being uncomfortable. However, I equally feared the idea of finding comfort. I used to think I could handle things on my own, especially my own mental health.

I soon discovered that I needed others to help me understand myself. Processing past experiences help us face our fear. Throughout my journey, I forgot my past experiences. I had so much pride that I needed my life to stay the same – my family structure, my friendships, and external experiences I used to define my life. Oddly enough, I viewed myself as being so humble that I didn't think I needed to change anything about my thought processes. I am an animal of nature. I have the unusual desire to learn more about myself everyday, regardless of how uncomfortable it requires me to be.

In college, I was thrown into the most uncomfortable circumstance of my young adult life. I was so prideful that I didn't change anything, I simply adjusted to my new life. My pride had finally overcome my humility and I became uncomfortable with myself. I was so uncomfortable with myself that I went into what is called a psychosis state. For me, it was simply a state of isolation. I isolated myself from my friends and family; those that I love and live for. I was alone – by choice. Even still, I couldn't comprehend why I felt so alone. My own pride was clouding my judgment – and I remained clueless, empty, alone and unhappy. So, I continued believing that nothing in my life needed to change. The more uncomfortable I became with myself, the more I sought answers to questions that seemed to have no real answer.

I began to study every religion I could think of, literally. It made me realize that they all had the same ending. The books all ends on a good note – they simply just end. I didn't understand why they all just ended. As a result, I became angry trying to search for the answers. However, the journey was mentally exhausting and extremely uncomfortable. I was unable to face myself in the mirror, until I got to know myself. I needed self-assurance. Facing myself became my biggest fear. The mirror is proof of our existence, yet it became my biggest fear. After facing this fear repeatedly, I found an answer. What deems our hierarchy in the animal kingdom is forgetting that humans are merely animals in nature. Otherwise, we are more like savages.

We all have the same basic fears; of which we forgive ourselves. This superficial boldness allows us to feel comfortable. I forgot that I was just as good as everyone else, because I refused to look in a mirror. I was prideful. Now, I've learned that pride comes before the fall. Pride is an evil good. Pride allows people to be comfortable doing anything they desire. It also blinds individuals from doing more then they can. The reason animals don't change is because they are comfortable with there existence. *Mi Own Collection* allowed me to realize that I could be comfortable, if I dealt with my discomforts. Mental health support taught me how to overcome the poisonous pride that was pulling me into a dark hole.

RE-EXPLANATION III

I always feared doctors. The historian is the person that knows you the best. Let me explain. Everything good and bad about our existence lies with a box. Inside that box is nothing but a mirror. The evil isn't that you opened the box. We should choose to see ourselves. The evil is based on our intentions when we open the box – our motives define us. Belief systems are scary to everybody, because we all want to be perfectly comfortable with ourselves. We all want to believe that we only do what is right. Nobody wants to be wrong. For me, belief was literally my greatest fear. I didn't want to believe that someone knew me better than I knew myself. However, my greatest fear turned into my biggest relief. Doctor Hope is the person we aim to be most like, because he gives our future added meaning.

Don't fear yourself – don't even let your greatest fear be that you are powerful beyond measure. The devil is the personification of our own evil limitations. The only way to understand clearly is to divide this concept into two parts. First, accepting Doctor Hope as the person we want to be most like. Secondly, it is important to trust that others can know you better than yourself. That's how you break away from every box.

RE-EXPLANATION IV

Talk amongst yourselves. Be open for discussion. Have confidence, hope and faith. Always remember to smile. Have as much fun as possible without bothering others. Never forget that laughter is medicine.

RE-EXPLANTION V

We all chose to live within our own understanding, but some

people chose to see the objective truth. Now, I can see clearly again. *Mi Own* time is always about living in the now – living in the moment. Who are you? Whether you know the answer to that question or not, you are important. It took some very important people in my life to convince me just how important I am. I am dedicated to the people who make me believe I can accomplish anything I set my mind to. Everything in life is a choice, and I chose to remember my mistakes – they are the proof that I am a perfectly flawed human being. I am not purely perfect; however, I am wonderfully made. This book allows readers to travel through my experiences. If used properly, it will transform into your own personal time machine that will transport and teleport you to new dimensions of life and dispensation of time. Find F.U.N. on your ingenious *Mi Own* journey.

MI OWN JOURNAL

Use this MI OWN journal section to write your own thoughts concerning **MY UNDERSTANDING**, *The Humble Prideful Oxymoron.*

_____

_____

_____

_____

_____

_____

2 HOUR HOUSE
Leadership from the Ground Up

Brian Conaway
with Jose Feliciano

**Leadership from
the Ground Up**